Disney SONGS FOR TWO

Disney Characters and Artwork
TM & © 2018 Disney

*TARZAN® Owned by Edgar Rice Burroughs, Inc.
And Used by Permission
© Burroughs/Disney

The following songs are the property of:

Bourne Co.
Music Publishers
5 West 37th Street
New York, NY 10018

HEIGH-HO
SOME DAY MY PRINCE WILL COME
WHEN YOU WISH UPON A STAR
WHISTLE WHILE YOU WORK
WHO'S AFRAID OF THE BIG BAD WOLF?

Arrangements by Mark Phillips

ISBN 978-1-5400-3708-4

Visit Hal Leonard Online at
www.halleonard.com

Contact Us:
Hal Leonard
7777 West Bluemound Road
Milwaukee, WI 53213
Email: info@halleonard.com

In Europe contact:
Hal Leonard Europe Limited
42 Wigmore Street
Marylebone, London, W1U 2RN
Email: info@halleonardeurope.com

In Australia contact:
Hal Leonard Australia Pty. Ltd.
4 Lentara Court
Cheltenham, Victoria, 3192 Australia
Email: info@halleonard.com.au

BEAUTY AND THE BEAST
from BEAUTY AND THE BEAST

FLUTES

Music by ALAN MENKEN
Lyrics by HOWARD ASHMAN

Moderately slow

BIBBIDI-BOBBIDI-BOO
(The Magic Song)

from CINDERELLA

Words by JERRY LIVINGSTON
Music by MACK DAVID
and AL HOFFMAN

FLUTES

Brightly, in 2

CAN YOU FEEL THE LOVE TONIGHT

from THE LION KING

FLUTES

Music by ELTON JOHN
Lyrics by TIM RICE

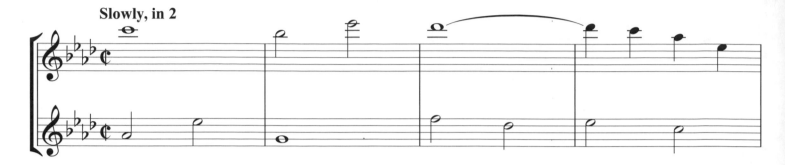

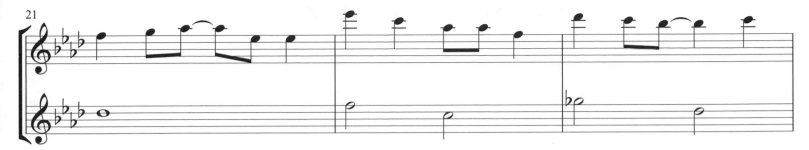

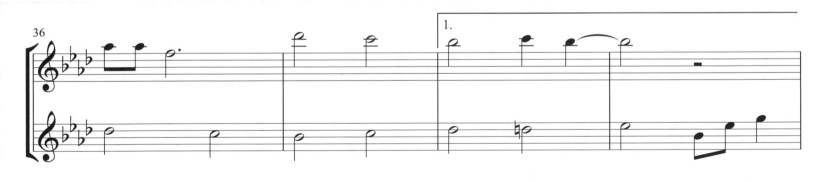

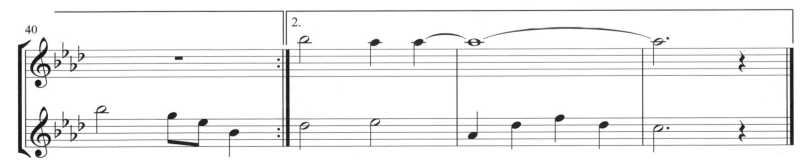

CHIM CHIM CHER-EE

from MARY POPPINS

Words and Music by RICHARD M. SHERMAN
and ROBERT B. SHERMAN

FLUTES

CIRCLE OF LIFE

from THE LION KING

Music by ELTON JOHN
Lyrics by TIM RICE

FLUTES

Moderately slow

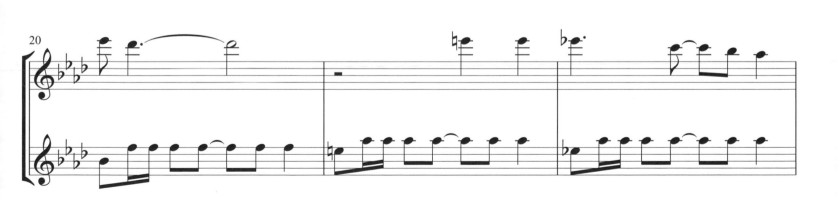

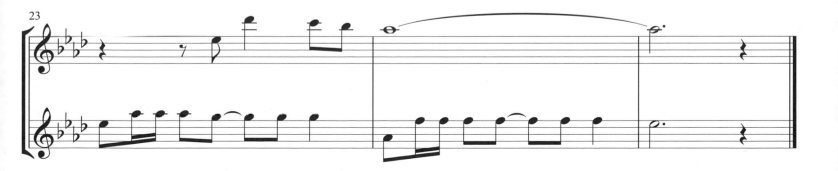

COLORS OF THE WIND

from POCAHONTAS

FLUTES

Music by ALAN MENKEN
Lyrics by STEPHEN SCHWARTZ

Moderately

EVERMORE
from BEAUTY AND THE BEAST

FLUTES

Music by ALAN MENKEN
Lyrics by TIM RICE

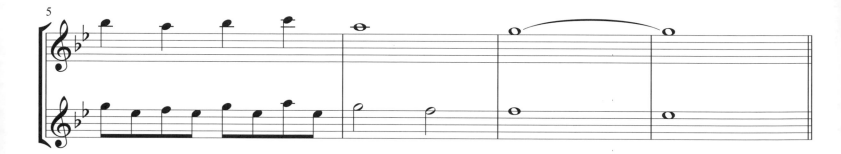

FRIEND LIKE ME

from ALADDIN

FLUTES

Music by ALAN MENKEN
Lyrics by HOWARD ASHMAN

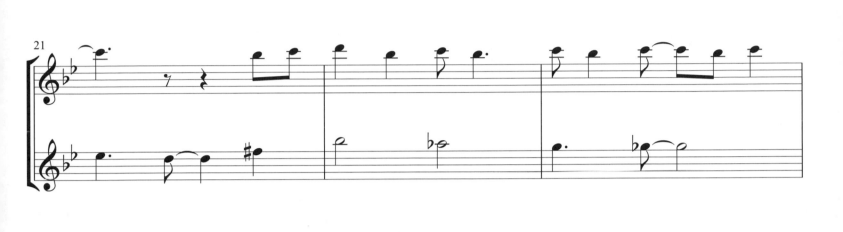

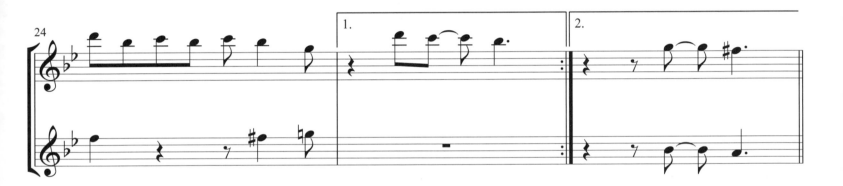

HEIGH-HO
The Dwarfs' Marching Song from SNOW WHITE AND THE SEVEN DWARFS

FLUTES

Words by LARRY MOREY
Music by FRANK CHURCHILL

HOW FAR I'LL GO

from MOANA

FLUTES

Music and Lyrics by
LIN-MANUEL MIRANDA

Moderately, in 2

LET IT GO
from FROZEN

FLUTES

Music and Lyrics by KRISTEN ANDERSON-LOPEZ
and ROBERT LOPEZ

MICKEY MOUSE MARCH

from THE MICKEY MOUSE CLUB

FLUTES

Words and Music by
JIMMIE DODD

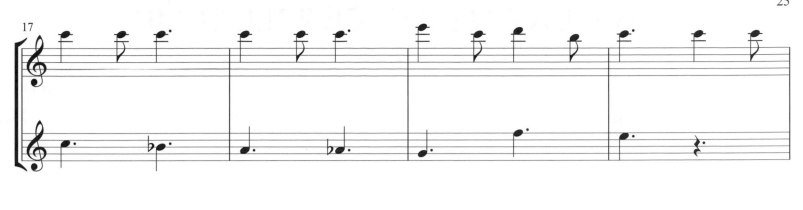

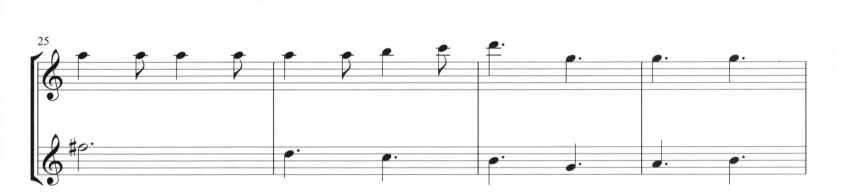

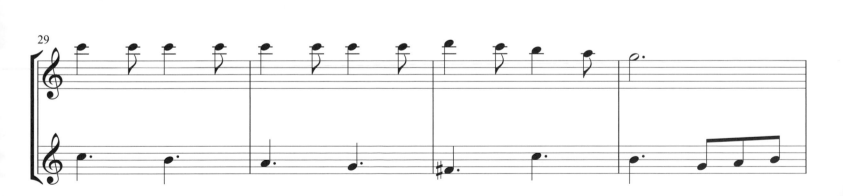

SOME DAY MY PRINCE WILL COME

from SNOW WHITE AND THE SEVEN DWARFS

Words by LARRY MOREY
Music by FRANK CHURCHILL

FLUTES

SOMETHING THERE

from BEAUTY AND THE BEAST

FLUTES

Music by ALAN MENKEN
Lyrics by HOWARD ASHMAN

Moderately fast

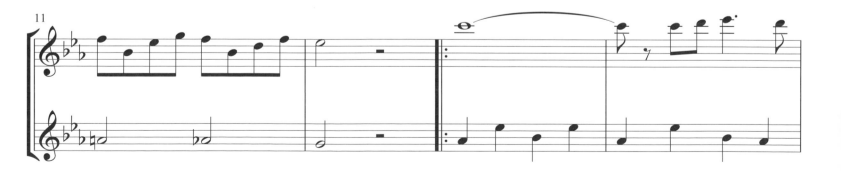

SUPERCALIFRAGILISTICEXPIALIDOCIOUS

from MARY POPPINS

FLUTES

Words and Music by RICHARD M. SHERMAN
and ROBERT B. SHERMAN

Fast, in 2

D.C. al Fine

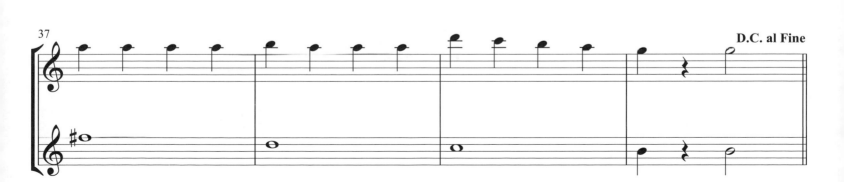

WHEN SHE LOVED ME

from TOY STORY 2

FLUTES

Music and Lyrics by
RANDY NEWMAN

Moderately slow, tenderly

WHEN YOU WISH UPON A STAR

from PINOCCHIO

FLUTES

Words by NED WASHINGTON
Music by LEIGH HARLINE

WHISTLE WHILE YOU WORK
from SNOW WHITE AND THE SEVEN DWARFS

FLUTES

Words by LARRY MOREY
Music by FRANK CHURCHILL

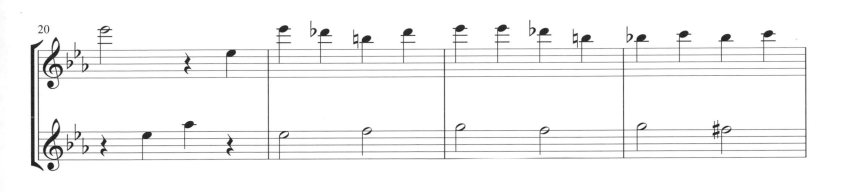

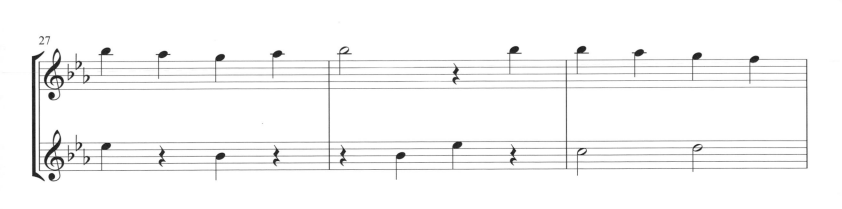

WHO'S AFRAID OF THE BIG BAD WOLF?

from THREE LITTLE PIGS

FLUTES

Words and Music by
FRANK CHURCHILL
Additional Lyric by ANN RONELL

Moderately, in 2

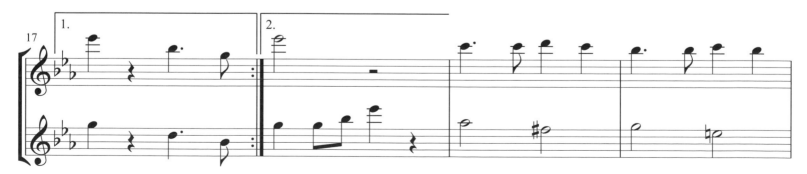

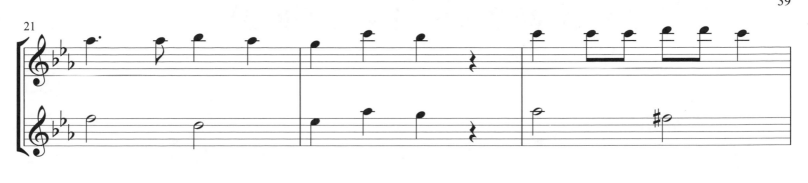

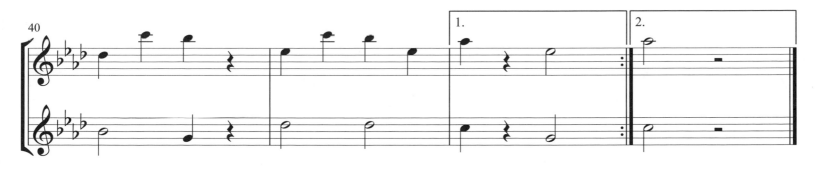

A WHOLE NEW WORLD

from ALADDIN

FLUTES

Music by ALAN MENKEN
Lyrics by TIM RICE

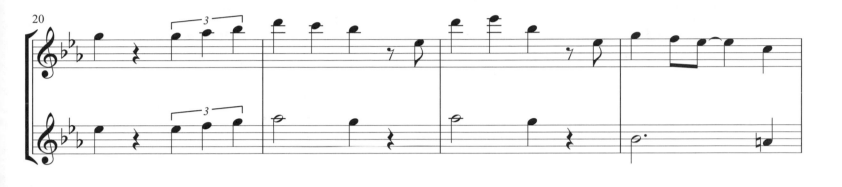

YOU'LL BE IN MY HEART

(Pop Version)

from TARZAN®

Flutes

Words and Music by
PHIL COLLINS

Moderately

YOU'RE WELCOME

from MOANA

FLUTES

Music and Lyrics by
LIN-MANUEL MIRANDA

ZIP-A-DEE-DOO-DAH

from SONG OF THE SOUTH

Words by RAY GILBERT
Music by ALLIE WRUBEL

FLUTES

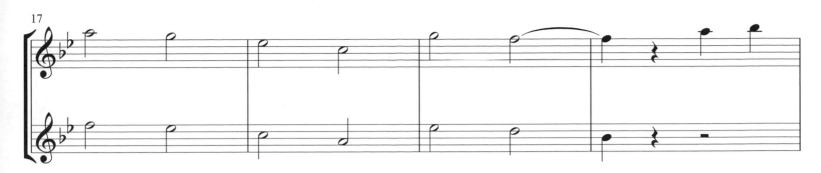